to Spot

Illustrated by Stephanie Fizer Coleman

Designed by Jenny Brown

Words by Sam Smith and
Kirsteen Robson

You can use the stickers to fill in the chart
at the back of the book, so you can keep
track of the insects you have seen.

The months in the description for each creature show
the time of year when you are most likely to see it.

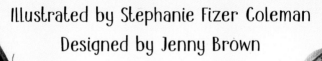

Gardens

7-spot ladybird

Look in gardens, hedges, woods and meadows. Hibernates during colder months in cracks in sheds, houses or tree bark. March-October.

Buff-tailed bumblebee

Buzzes between flowers in summer, feeding on nectar. Also collects pollen, in tiny yellow pouches on its legs. February-October.

Small tortoiseshell butterfly

Wakes from hibernation in spring. Females lay big heaps of eggs on the underside of nettle leaves. Visits many flowers. March-November.

Green lacewing

Found in gardens and hedges.
Sometimes attracted inside by
house lights. Hibernates in
sheds or houses. April-October.

Garden tiger moth

Mostly active at night. Its
caterpillars are fuzzy and may
make your skin itch, so don't
touch them. June-September.

caterpillar is called
a woolly bear.

Devil's coach horse beetle

Comes out at night. Rests in leaf litter
or under stones in the day. Lifts tail
and spreads jaws if threatened.
April-October.

3

Gardens

Peacock butterfly

'Eye' markings on wings help
to scare enemies. Looks like
a dead leaf when wings are
shut. All year round.

Common earwig

Sleeps during day in damp places
such as under stones. Comes out
at night to feed. All year round.

Black ant

Scuttles around collecting food.
Males and queens have wings. They
fly out of the nest in mid-summer
to mate, then the queens form new
colonies. June-August.

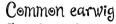

4

Bee fly
Uses its long mouthparts to drink nectar from flowers. Lays eggs near bees' nests. When the eggs hatch, the grubs eat the bee grubs. April-June.

Red admiral butterfly
Often seen collecting nectar from flowering ivy and Michaelmas daisies. May-October.

Hoverfly
Black and yellow markings make it look like a wasp but it doesn't sting. Often hovers in the air without moving. March-November.

Towns and parks

Common wasp
Yellow and black striped body with a pointed end. Feeds on sweet foods and liquids and other insects. Most likely to sting in late summer. April-October.

Small white butterfly
Underwings are creamy white. Lays single eggs on cabbages and Brussels sprouts. May and August.

Vapourer moth
Males have rusty brown wings with two white spots. Females only have wing stubs and can't fly. July-September.

Cinnabar moth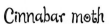

Sometimes flies in the day as well as at night. Look on waste ground and railway banks. May-August.

Cockchafer or Maybug

Flies around treetops. Sometimes flies down chimneys and against lighted windows. April-June.

22-spot ladybird

Very small. Eats mould that grows on soil and low-growing plants. April-August.

Trees and woodlands

Stag beetle
Male has large jaws that look like antlers. Most common in southern England. May-September.

Horse fly
Female sucks blood, but her loud hum usually warns you before you are bitten. May-September.

Hornet
Stinging insect larger than a wasp. Stripes are orange-yellow and brown. Nests in hollow trees, banks or roofs. May-November.

Green shieldbug

Lives on trees such as hazel
and birch. Bright green
in spring. Green-bronze
later. May-October.

Violet ground beetle

Rests during the day in leaf
litter or under logs or stones.
Eats other insects, slugs and
worms. March-October.

Horned treehopper

Thorny-looking bugs that jump
along twigs and low plants in
woods. Feeds on oak leaves and
other plants. April-August.

9

Trees and woodlands

Poplar hawk moth

Wings are sometimes purplish.
Front wings stick out over
back wings while it rests.
May-August.

Peach blossom moth

Name comes from the peach
blossom pattern on its wings.
Flies at night. Attracted to light
and sugar. June-September.

Herald moth

Flies at night and rests among
dead leaves by day. Look for the
bright orange patches on its
wings. March-November.

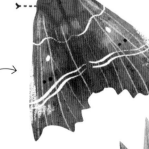

Purple emperor butterfly

Large, purple-tinged males fly around treetops. Drinks from woodland puddles. July-August.

Wasp beetle

Looks similar to a wasp and behaves the same way, but is harmless. Flies in bright sunshine, visiting flowers. May-August.

Red-headed cardinal beetle

Look for it sunbathing on flowers, tree trunks and stumps, where it also hunts other insects. May-July.

Meadows and grasslands

Field grasshopper
Males 'chirrup' as they rub their legs against their wings. Look in short vegetation on sunny days. May-October.

Glow worm
Wingless females sit on blades of grass at dusk and attract males with their glowing tails. May-August.

Female glow worm

Ghost moth
Males often seen at dusk searching for yellow-winged females in dense grass. June-July.

Common blue butterfly

Males are blue. Females, blue or brown. Active on sunny days. Rests head-down on blades of grass when it's cloudy or wet. June-September.

Green tortoise beetle

Pulls its legs and antennae in when threatened, so it looks like a tiny tortoise. Food plants include white dead-nettles. April-October.

Dor beetle

Flies at night with a loud droning sound to dung heaps, where it eats its own weight in dung. April-October.

13

Meadows and grasslands

Black and red froghopper
Holds its wing cases up to form
a tent shape over its body while
it rests. Look in dense grass
and on trees. April-June.

Common malachite beetle
Look in buttercups and other flowers.
Smelly orange pouches bulge from
its sides when alarmed, to put off
enemies. April-August.

Green leafhopper
Feeds on grasses and rushes.
Males are turquoise or black.
Females are green. Communicates
with faint clicks. May-September.

Meadow brown butterfly

Visits thistles and bramble flowers, even on dull days. Females have large orange patches on each of their four wings. June-September.

Marbled white butterfly

Look for it on purple flowers such as thistles, knapweed and field scabious. June-August.

Oil beetle

This large beetle can't fly, so is often trodden on as it walks along paths and clifftops. Oozes drops of oily liquid when alarmed. March-May.

Ponds and lakes

Backswimmer

Lives in pools, canals and ditches. Jerks along with hind legs, usually on its back. Eats tadpoles and small fish. All year round.

Pond skater

'Skates' across the water's surface. Picks up dead or dying insects with its short front legs. April-October.

Water measurer

Edges of ponds, slow rivers and streams. Stabs mosquito larvae (young) and water fleas with its sharp mouthparts. Also eats dead insects. All year round.

Whirligig beetle
Gathers in groups on surface of still or slow-moving water in bright sunshine. Swims in frantic circles, and dives underwater if disturbed. July-September.

Common blue damselfly
Look in vegetation near water. Female's body is duller blue or green, with black stripes. April-September.

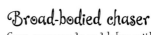

Broad-bodied chaser
Seen over ponds and lakes with plenty of plants. Flies in short bursts in search of insects, and often returns to same perch. May-August.

Rivers and wetlands

Mayfly

Adult lives are short,
often only a few hours.
In this time they mate, and
females lays their eggs on the
water's surface. All year round. ↗

Banded demoiselle

Males perch on plants by water and
flutter their wings to attract a mate.
Lives by canals, streams and rivers
with muddy bottoms. May-August.

Golden-ringed dragonfly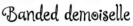

Fast and powerful flier. Lives near
streams and rivers, but is sometimes
seen far from water. May-September.

Emperor dragonfly

Seen over large ponds, lakes and canals. Female is dull green. Adults catch flies in flight. June-October.

Giant crane fly

Often found near water. Related to 'Daddy-long-legs'. These weak fliers wobble about in the air. April-August.

Yellow brimstone butterfly

Leaf-shaped wings give camouflage when resting on plants and hedges. Female is pale greeny-white. All year round.

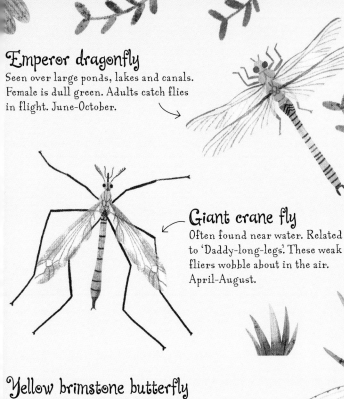

Heaths and moors

Heath assassin bug

Look on open heaths and sand dunes. Sucks body fluids out of prey. Most adults are wingless. June-October.

Green tiger beetle

Runs quickly and flies, buzzing, for short distances if disturbed. April-September.

Minotaur beetle

Has three bull-like horns. Found in sandy places where rabbits live. Eats rabbit dung. September-July.

Emperor moth

Males fly around quickly during the day. Females rest on low plants. March-May.

Silver-studded blue butterfly

Visits heather. Males are blue. Females are brown. June-August.

Large heath butterfly

Visits heath flowers, rests on grasses with wings closed if the weather is too warm, sunny or windy. June-August.

Spotting chart

Once you've spotted an insect from this book, find its sticker at the back, and stick it on this chart in the space below its name.

7-spot ladybird	22-spot ladybird	Backswimmer	Banded demoiselle	Bee fly
Black and red froghopper	Black ant	Broad-bodied chaser	Buff-tailed bumblebee	Cinnabar moth
Cockchafer	Common blue butterfly	Common blue damselfly	Common earwig	Common malachite beet*
Common wasp	Devil's coach horse beetle	Dor beetle	Emperor dragonfly	Emperor moth
Field grasshopper	Garden tiger moth	Ghost moth	Giant crane fly	Glow worm

Golden-ringed dragonfly	Green lacewing	Green leafhopper	Green shieldbug	Green tiger beetle
Green tortoise beetle	Heath assassin bug	Herald moth	Horned treehopper	Hornet
Horse fly	Hoverfly	Large heath butterfly	Marbled white butterfly	Mayfly
Meadow brown butterfly	Minotaur beetle	Oil beetle	Peach blossom moth	Peacock butterfly
Pond skater	Poplar hawk moth	Purple emperor butterfly	Red admiral butterfly	Red-headed cardinal beetle
Silver-studded blue butterfly	Small tortoise-shell butterfly	Small white butterfly	Stag beetle	Vapourer moth
Violet ground beetle	Wasp beetle	Water measurer	Whirligig beetle	Yellow brimstone butterfly

Index